CAREER COMBAT

*To Leigh Lichtenegger
Congratulations and best wishes on your graduation.
Col. Alex V. Faval
27 Nov 99*

CAREER COMBAT

A Field Manual for
Winning and Advancing in
the American Workplace

Colonel Alexander V. Farol

Castle
Pacific
Publishing

Washington, DC

Copyright © 1999
Col. Alex Farol
c/o Castle Pacific Publishing
Washington, DC
www.castlepacific.com

All rights reserved
Manufactured in the United States of America
First printing December 1999

ISBN 0-9653869-5-3
Library of Congress Catalog Card Number 98-76209

CONTENTS

PREFACE 1
INTRODUCTION 3

PART ONE: PERFORMANCE

1. Delivering the Goods 11
2. Translating Potential into Performance 17
3. Conditions on the Battlefield 27
4. The Past is Prologue 35
Key Points 39

PART TWO: RELATIONSHIPS

5. The Human Condition 43
6. Who you Know 49
7. Know the Players 57
8. Assessing the Costs and Benefits 65
Key Points 72

PART THREE: OPPORTUNITIES

9. Recognizing Opportunity 75
10. Preparing for Battle 79
11. Nothing Ventured, Nothing Gained 87
12. Your Move 93
Key Points 98

CLOSING THOUGHTS 101
NOTES 103

PREFACE

THE LOST ART OF CAREER-BUILDING

My motive in writing this book is very simple. I have observed that many young people are confused by the American workplace, unable to find a place in the ranks, and (if they are so lucky as to find work) unable to make much progress despite hard work. Because I am both an observer and an activist, I tried to understand what factors made some careers successful while others stagnated. The result, after fifteen years of ruminations, is this book. Its sole reason for being is to help those seeking jobs to get them, and those having jobs to develop rewarding and productive careers from them.

Since I intend that *Career Combat* should not just grace bookshelves, but be used actively "in the field," I decided that the subtitle for this book should incorporate the name "field manual," known affectionately by soldiers as an "FM." Like all field manuals, this one should be consulted when needed to address operational problems—like building your career.

Very Sincerely,

Alex V. Farol

Col. Alexander V. Farol

In order that people may be happy
in their work, these three things are
needed: They must be fit for it.
They must not do too much of it.
And they must have a sense of
success in it.

John Ruskin
1819–1900

INTRODUCTION

LAYING THE GROUNDWORK

SECTION 1: COMBAT AND YOUR CAREER

In the early nineteenth century the Prussian general and military philosopher, Karl von Clausewitz, observed that the practice of war—as opposed to the theory and planning for warfare—was filled with chaos, chance, and uncertainty. In Clausewitz's view, the only lamps capable of illuminating the fog of war were the human factors of courage, effort, good judgment, persistence, determination, and luck.

Work, like war, is also highly chaotic. Despite its theoretical portrayal as an orderly, rational, even predictable environment, the real workplace is a battlefield which is also filled with chaos, chance, and uncertainty. And like war, the only lamps capable of illuminating the fog of the workplace are courage, effort, good judgment, persistence, determination, and luck.

This field manual was written to help you discover and develop your "lamps"—your tools for surviving and succeeding in the American workplace. Its objectives are to:
- prepare you for combat, and keep you on the battlefield while you gain some combat experience;
- help you muster courage in the face of difficulties and setbacks, and convince you that—with some combat experience—you can win;

- describe some realities of the American workplace and present some ideas about how to cope; and
- stimulate your own thinking.

In the three sections of this manual we will touch on vital skills that you can use in your daily battle in the workplace. These include many old, familiar topics like time management and perseverance, and one or two "new" ideas. But, old or new, the material is presented in an *operational* context—that is, the ideas are presented in such a way that they can be put to immediate use in planning and conducting your campaign to gain employment or promotion. It is the *operational* perspective which will enable you to make practical use of values and qualities which would otherwise be moot.

SECTION 2: JOBS AND CAREERS

If you are a young man or woman just entering the workforce, the first thing you must know is the difference between a "job" and a "career." Even though you may be looking for a job, be advised that you are also beginning your career. And the career you build will absorb the greater part of your working life.

The word "job" comes from an old Anglo-Saxon word meaning a lump or piece. Figuratively, "job" gives a sense of something done which is well-defined, well known, and of finite duration. As one job is taken up, another is left behind.

A "career," however, implies something unlimited and in motion. From the French "carrière," meaning a road or highway, a career may be poorly known but for the immediate future. Like many roads, a career is filled with twists and turns, detours and byways, potholes and washed-out bridges. But, whatever its condition, a career leads onward through unknown lands, and may take you to a destination far from where you started.

The job you have today, or are seeking, is important. But it is only the first step in a lifelong journey.

In recent years there has been a trend away from building thirty-year careers in just one organization. Today the pattern seems to be movement between a succession of organizations. This is partly due to a "throw-away" mentality on the part of senior executives anxious to squeeze organizations for their contents, and then throw away the rinds. Many organizations simply don't last thirty years. Also, young people may be more adventurous and possibly more willing to accept change and risk than their elders. With good reason, their view of the workplace is more tentative and skeptical than was the case in past generations. The new generation may choose a series of short pulls rather than a long haul. But that still adds up to a career.

SECTION 3: BUILDING A CAREER

Career-building is very much the "art of the possible." True, not all things are possible—even in a country which prides itself that boys born in log cabins, like Booker T. Washington or Abraham Lincoln, may become great educators or presidents. But there are discernible factors that play decisive roles in making possible the development of careers—three, in fact.

Careers appear to be built upon the interplay of *performance*, *relationships*, and *opportunities*. These three factors appear interrelated, for the absence of any one seriously checks the possibility of a successful career.

Performance is the essential starting point of a successful career. But it is only a start. Without good relationships in the workplace and elsewhere, and timely opportunities fully exploited, even the best of performers will go nowhere—slowly. Taken together, however, they lead to advancement, excitement, and challenge.

Later, as careers begin to develop, *performance*, *relationships*, and *opportunities* form a kaleidoscopic pattern in which each factor enhances the other two. Demonstrated competent performance will establish the basis for a wide circle of professional relationships. In turn, your relationships help you identify and capture more and better opportunities. And, properly seized upon, opportunities become the means for demonstrating your capability to perform at higher levels of skill or responsibility while widening your circle of relationships. Once set in motion—and unless disrupted—the PRO cycle is dynamic.

SECTION 4: WHAT IS REQUIRED

Doesn't that make it sound easy? Yes, unfortunately, it does. Too easy. And, rest assured, building a career is not easy. The next thirty years will be rough. Unless you lead a charmed life, marry the boss's son or daughter, or inherit the company from a relative, you will suffer frustrations, setbacks, bad luck, and discouragement like the rest of us. You will make mistakes. Bad judgment will cost you opportunities—and maybe even friends. The American workplace is no place for cowards, and it certainly is no place for fools.

But never doubt for a moment that however tough things may be, you are capable of great heroism. True heroism is nothing more than the courage of the human spirit to struggle on despite obstacles and failures, and trying to succeed despite fearful odds. What is required of you is determination and self-discipline of a high order.

Whatever your talent and experience, whatever your background and education, whatever the glory and danger before you, the three factors of *performance, relationships,* and *opportunities* are constants—compass points along your career path.

Getting started (or restarted) in a career is always tough. The beginning of any undertaking is always the most difficult phase. It is also the most important. But, as the Chinese sages observed, "Even a journey of ten thousand *li* begins with but a single step." Get started now. Apply whatever seems helpful to you from this field manual. Put on the armor of courage and optimism as you go into battle.

The thing to keep in mind is persistence. Even in this time of corporate downsizing and government funding cutbacks, there is something out there for you. Finding it may not be easy, but it is there to be found. So—don't become discouraged. And never lose your optimism, things will eventually work out.

Skeptics may reject these Pollyannish statements out of hand. If you have a fundamentally pessimistic attitude, you can be sure of one thing: *you won't find anything out there*. This is because you won't make much of an effort to look—after all, you've already decided there is nothing to find. Pessimism is a self-fulfilling prophecy.

Yet the argument for optimism is compelling, because it is based on experience and observation. If you are willing to seek, you will eventually find. Other generations in other times—*and in times much worse than these*—have succeeded in their search.

A final thought before you begin: remember that whatever your work—mechanic, file clerk, secretary, soldier or account executive—*you are a professional*. As such, you are captain of your own career.

> Professionals make the difficult look easy—they do so cheerfully and without fanfare. But it is the constant striving for improvement, for perfection in a highly imperfect world, that truly distinguishes the professional from all others.

PART ONE: PERFORMANCE

By the work one knows the workman.

Jean de la Fontaine
1621–1695

A great pilot can sail even when his canvas is rent.

Seneca

ONE

DELIVERING THE GOODS

SECTION 5: PERFORMANCE AND RESULTS

Make no mistake: bosses like people who do good work. There is cynicism, of course, about those who get ahead without having to work. In some cases, the cynicism is fully justified. We all know examples of nincompoops who are given weighty responsibilities and high positions for which they are woefully unfit.

But not in most cases. The majority of career successes depend upon a solid record of achievement—*performance*. Performance is the consistent delivery of desired results. Put another, perhaps more military way, it is the accomplishment of one's assigned mission. This is true of any occupation you can think of: a merchant who delivers quality goods at competitive prices, a craftsman who provides timely, excellent services, a manager who brings in higher profits, a plumber you don't have to call twice, or a military commander who consistently wins battles. "By the work one knows the workman."

In the American system—which is otherwise chaotic and volatile—one thing is rock firm: the demand for results. Unlike some foreign societies, where family pedigree and accident of birth compensate for lack of demonstrable results, such is not the case in America. Americans typically ask, "What can you *do*?" More importantly, American bosses ask, "What have you done for me *lately*?"

Why? It's probably because, since Jamestown and Plymouth Rock, results were the measure not only of success, but of survival. The point is that, for Americans, work is serious business. Now, work may be exciting and challenging, even fun. But whatever else it may be, it is always serious business. And results are the measure of work.

SECTION 6: COMPETITION AND COMPARISON

There is another fact of life in the American workplace: competition. Always remember that in the wilderness of the workplace, you're all alone. Your work will be constantly compared and evaluated with that of others. Like it or not, you're a competitor.

Competition and comparison, in fact, seem etched into the American brain. Phrases such as "more than, better than, quicker than, and cheaper than" dominate American advertising, annual reports, sales presentations, and performance evaluations. Charles Darwin was absolutely correct when he described life as a struggle for existence. Certainly his observation is true of the American workplace. The frightening reality is that you—and you alone—must compete and struggle for professional existence with all others. Every day.

You know the simple calculus that "if John does ten accounts per day, and Jane does fifteen equally well," Jane is the better performer. "If George sells good hamburgers, but Sam's are better," Sam is the stronger competitor.

Competition, battle, and struggle, then, are the order of the day in the American workplace. Make no mistake—the workplace is not fair—and never has been. Even in a court of law, the guilty often walk and the innocent occasionally are convicted. This is not because of some abstract fairness, but because of the rough and tumble of legal combat in the courtroom. One attorney is trying hard to put the defendant in jail, while opposing counsel is trying equally hard to keep him out. Competition, battle, and struggle will determine the outcome. Fairness has nothing to do with it.

Remember also that you are not only a competitor with others, but most importantly, with yourself. The better you perform, the more is expected of you. You must continually raise your level of performance. In America, today's high achievement becomes tomorrow's standard.

SECTION 7: PRODUCTIVITY

America is a productive society. It may be that competition, whether ferocious or genteel, is the engine of productivity. Past empires were predatory or contemplative—and almost always rigidly hierarchical. America, over its short history, has been incredibly productive—and basically egalitarian. But highly competitive. If you have a new invention that people want to buy, you'll find yourself president of your own corporation and on your way to your first million. And, like Bill Gates, you don't have to wear a tie to work if you don't want to, as long as you can beat the competition.

The point is that your performance—and your comparison with the performance of others—is the cornerstone of each job you hold. Remember that your competitors are trying to outperform *you*, every day. The real question is, "Can you deliver exactly *what* is needed *when* it is needed? Consistently?" If the organization's needs are well-served—whether profits earned, services provided, or victories won—you have delivered what the American system demands: Results.

A demonstrated track record of superior performance is the essential basis of a successful career. Remember that it is the *expectation* you will perform well that will land you the job or the promotion. It is the documented *fulfillment* of those expectations by solid performance that allows you to hold the job and justify the promotion. But performance by itself is not sufficient. Just because you work hard does not necessarily mean you will advance. As you will see, other factors are also necessary for success.

It's not what cards you hold, it's how well you play those you hold.

Josh Billings
1818–1885

We know what we are, but know not what we may be.

Shakespeare
Hamlet

TWO

TRANSLATING POTENTIAL INTO PERFORMANCE

SECTION 8: TALENT VS COMPETENCY

Sad to say, talent is valueless by itself. To have value, talent must be transformed into achievement. Talent is merely a kind of potential waiting for concrete form and definition. Competency, on the other hand, is actual, demonstrated proficiency. It is talent made manifest.

Transforming potential into actual performance is one of the greatest challenges you face in the workplace battleground. This is for two reasons. First, you may not even know what you are capable of. But second, even if you *do* know what you can do, you still need an opportunity to show your stuff. Frankly, from the point of view of a boss who doesn't know you, you're dangerous. After all, why should he or she risk the company's profit margin—not to mention his or her professional reputation—to gamble that this unknown new kid (you) can perform? If the boss gambles on you—and you blow it—he or she knows whose neck will be on the block for the bone-headed hiring decision.

Your situation is kind of like the new third string football player on the bench begging the coach to send him in when the Army team is trailing Navy by six points in the fourth quarter. Unless the coach has a compelling reason for sending the new kid in, the kid will sit on the bench for the rest of the game.

Coaches, bosses, political leaders, and commanders always want to place a safe bet, especially in tight circumstances where the stakes are high. After all, in the real world you play for keeps. This means they will always go with the known quantity, the proven performer. Such proven performers often become favorites—and the overuse of favorites tends to choke off opportunities for new talent. This is unfortunate. But it is also a fact of life. In the face of obstacles, you will need ingenuity and perseverance to convert your talent into demonstrated proficiency.

SECTION 9: "KNOW THYSELF"

Well, we're not here to whine, but to get you off the bench and into the game. The solution to this problem lies within yourself. And the key is to know yourself very well—indeed, to be brutally honest with yourself in terms of your skills and aptitudes as well as your weaknesses and shortcomings. You must know where you can perform competitively.

Every human being has a unique collage of strengths and weaknesses. Some people are good at math, while others may have special talent for graphic arts. Some people are great cooks, but couldn't find their way from Hackensack to Hoboken with a road map, street signs, and directions if their lives depended on it. The point is, you have a unique mixture of things you do well and enjoy doing. Likewise, there are things you do poorly—and would just as soon avoid. Don't brood about the talents your neighbor has that you lack. Play the cards you do have—and make the most of the hand you've been dealt.

SECTION 10: INVENTORY YOUR TALENTS AND ABILITIES

Look at yourself objectively. What are you good at? What do you enjoy doing? What have you done well in the past? Also, what would you *like* to do—if you only had the chance? List these things on a sheet of paper. Don't think about them at this point—just get them down. Don't quit until you have listed every "positive" you can think of.

When you have inventoried your positives, take a fresh sheet of paper and list the things you do *poorly*. What lies outside your expertise? Be honest. What would you avoid—if you could? List as many as you can think of. The more you list, the better able you will be to identify potential pitfalls to your career.

Then, group like items on both sheets. For example, let's say you enjoy visiting art museums, own a collection of illustrated books about French impressionist painters, and can't resist sketching almost anything in sight. A pattern begins to emerge here.

An objective comparison will identify proven abilities and possibly even hidden talent. You can refine your list and sharpen the results by weighting each item based on degree of skill or importance to you.

There is also a purely subjective weighting that must take place. Does a given option feel right, or satisfy? Consider the Russian composer Alexander

Borodin who, by all accounts, was a highly competent chemist and physician. However, by avocation, Borodin was a world-class composer. Why? Probably because that's where his heart was. The illegitimate son of a Georgian prince, Borodin was brought up by a Russian peasant family, and educated for a medical profession. Music was not considered a worthy profession—medicine was. Even though Borodin practiced medicine, he loved music. His works include the beautiful *Polovetsian Dances* from *Prince Igor, In the Steppes of Central Asia*, and several symphonies and other compositions—all of which he wrote in his spare time. Bear in mind that we remember Borodin today for his music, not for his medicine.

Though you should be objective in assessing yourself, you needn't be mechanistic. Self-assessment is not an exact science.

Get a friend who is a clear thinker with some imagination to go over the two lists with you. Try to associate aptitudes and skills with real-world activities. Focus on the positives. But keep the negatives nearby as a sanity check on your likely fitness for particular jobs. To the extent that your background matches with the requirements of a given job, you are more likely to succeed there. This is not guaranteed, of course. But it is a safer bet.

SECTION 11: EFFORT AND DETERMINATION

All the talent and aptitude in the world will do you no good without one indispensable ingredient—*effort*. Effort is the expenditure of physical or mental energy to achieve a desired result. To be sure, talents,

TRANSFORMING POTENTIAL INTO PERFORMANCE

skills, and education make it easier to achieve results. But you must never confuse *means*, such as education, skills, and talents, with *ends*—results. Results do not simply happen. They are achieved through determined, stubborn effort.

One such example of persistence and effort which transformed talent into achievement is the story of a man born of illiterate parents and raised in abject poverty. This young man thirsted for education and the desire to help others, and worked as a house servant, coal miner, and salt refiner while he acquired a primary education. Walking and hitching rides to get to Hampton, Virginia, where he was admitted to college, the young man worked nights as a janitor to put himself through school. Completing school, he held several teaching positions before founding the Tuskegee Institute. Booker T. Washington's hard work and commitment not only made him a man of education, but created opportunities for thousands of others to follow in his footsteps.

SECTION 12: SHOW WHAT YOU CAN DO

Focus on strengths. Build on known aptitudes and skills. Show just one person what you can do on the practice field before the big game. You needn't be spectacular, or make the play of the century. Rather, your consistent solid performance on the field—even if checkered by setbacks *which will occur*—is what will bring you to someone's notice.

Abraham Lincoln's long, hard road from desperate poverty and ignorance is well known. Almost everyone knows the story of Lincoln's work swinging an axe to split rails, and of stocking shelves and running errands at Berry's store. He gained a reputation for dependability, hard work, native intelligence, and wit. And for telling funny stories and winning friends.

But it was Lincoln's extraordinary gift for formulating and communicating ideas to others that enabled him to rise above his backwoods upbringing—despite some very tough breaks. Lincoln polished his communications skills in the courtroom and as a politician on the stump. Although his political career was marked by defeats as often as successes, Lincoln could articulate ideas as few men could. In the 1858 senatorial contest with Stephen A. Douglas, Lincoln lost the election but won national respect for his exceptional ability, including his famous warning to a nation on the brink of civil war that "a house divided against itself cannot stand."

Through the fiery trial of the American Civil War, Lincoln's great skills of conveying a vision through homely wit, lofty ideas, and plain talk, time and again inspired the American people. Lincoln's greatness can be seen in the words of his Gettysburg Address which captured both the grief and the hope of the tragic struggle, and the future which lay before America.

We may speculate on the consequences for America had Lincoln's neighbors in New Salem, Illinois, not noticed his great gift.

SECTION 13: ABILITY TO ADAPT

Don't be satisfied with your existing repertoire. Strive to acquire new competencies, and polish existing ones. The expansion of your capabilities brings a wider selection of opportunities within range. Likewise, a broad portfolio of professional skills gives you a greater chance of surviving adversity. Depth of expertise in a tiny area may help you survive, but the smart money rides on those with many arrows in their quivers.

Consider the extinction of the dinosaurs. Highly successful for 130 million years, well-adapted to their warm, swampy habitat, the dinos nonetheless had a fatal flaw. They were over-specialized. And their familiar habitat suddenly changed. The point is that inability to adapt to new conditions (whether due to complacency or failure to comprehend change) dooms one to occupational fossilization.

SECTION 14: INVEST IN YOURSELF

Experience is generally acknowledged to be the best teacher. Folk wisdom has it that "one learns by doing." This is certainly true, but it can also be painful. And, it assumes that you actually *learn from your mistakes*. The trial and error of experience results in mistakes and blind alleys as often as it leads to success and new learning. Even so, learning from experience is a life-long process, and a valuable part of one's personal and professional growth.

Learning from another's experience is equally valuable. Moreover, it is less time-consuming and usually less painful. This form of personal and professional growth takes two forms: education and training. Education, like experience, is a life-long process. Unlike experience, which comes to you, you must go in search of an education. Education consists of more than enrolling in a program of formal studies. In its broadest dimension, education is the development of the mind. It is the process of extending your memory and understanding through the acquisition of the experience and knowledge of others.

Training is more precisely defined as the acquisition of skills. Whereas education broadens your understanding, training teaches you how to do something. This may be the ability to jump the hurdles, play the trombone, learn to speak Russian, or draw a cartoon. Training is most effective if received from master practitioners. Good training is the shorthand of the master's hard-won experience. To get the full value of training, however, requires your intense commitment and desire to master the subject. You may have a natural aptitude to perform, but only if you are willing to put forth great effort can a great coach make you a star.

Clearly, you need both education and training. You must invest in both throughout your life. Obviously, they are most valuable when seasoned with your life experience which will grow with the passage of years. Above all, keep your eyes and ears open. As the ancient Chinese noted, "Wise men learn from other's mistakes, ordinary men from their own, and fools from neither."

I have nothing to offer but blood,
toil, tears, and sweat.

Churchill

For everything you have missed,
you have gained something else;
and for everything you gain, you
lose something else.

Emerson

THREE

CONDITIONS ON THE BATTLEFIELD

SECTION 15: OF CHAOS AND CONFUSION

We must now take a first glimpse at the battlefield. At one and the same time, it is commonplace, yet strange; familiar, yet puzzling; routine, yet treacherous. The workplace features all the conditions of the battlefield: chaos and confusion, friends and enemies, uncertainty and fear, tension, unpleasant surprises, and battle fatigue. There are also casualties and survivors, heroes and villains.

Yet the workplace also features many of the same virtues of the battlefield: Self-reliance, courage, initiative, perseverance, team play, leadership, and sacrifice.

First, it is important to realize that, despite a facade of Establishment Orderliness, the American workplace is chaotic—*highly chaotic*—and sometimes viciously so. This is because requirements are constantly changing, reorganizations are frequent, managerial leadership is constantly in flux, and new threats and opportunities appear almost daily. The vicissitudes of the workplace are legion: bankruptcies, hostile takeovers, powerful new competition, changes of Administration or national policy, downsizing and elimination of jobs, new bosses—the list is almost endless. But so it is in America, the land of permanent revolution. The only certainty is change.

New organizations rise phantom-like from the chaos, lumber forward a few yards or miles, stumble, and sink back into the mire. Even if the organization itself survives, the organization's mission and structure may be radically different a year from now than they are today. Consider, for example, the fate of famous airlines such as Pan Am or Eastern that once flew proudly. Today they are no more, and their people and aircraft are widely scattered. New lines have risen to take their places. How long will these new carriers last until they, too, pass away?

The question then becomes, "who can best adapt to a highly unstructured environment—especially one marked by conflict and struggle?"

It may be that people who are comfortable with ambiguity, and require little or no structure in their lives, are better suited for coping with the workplace than those of us who require some degree of structure, little ambiguity, and a predictable routine. Yet the reality is one of ambiguity and lack of structure. Corporate America's constantly-shifting priorities are shaped by larger forces—cutthroat competition, budget constraints, complex and often poorly-conceived projects—which those of us on the front lines may not fully understand. However, the unavoidable result for us soldiers in the trenches is turbulence, confusion, and uncertainty.

Whether or not this hypothesis is correct, it is most certainly true that one routinely sees in the job announcements and performance evaluations euphemisms such as "maintains flexibility on the job," and "adapts easily to rapidly changing priorities." These stock phrases are nothing more than clear signals of the underlying turbulence on the workplace battlefield. Since the chaos is not likely to abate anytime soon, worker flexibility will remain a key survival skill.

SECTION 16: TEAMS

One of the ancient mechanisms for dealing successfully with a hostile environment is the formation of teams. This has been true since Neolithic hunters discovered that teams had more success against mammoths than did individual spearmen. Now this is a major conundrum of the workplace battlefield: we are all competitors, all alone, and yet team play is essential to survival and victory. Like flexibility, we see the phrase "good team player" ballyhooed in job descriptions and annual appraisals.

Teams are a fact of life in modern organizations. Most are informal, *ad hoc* groupings which fold after serving some immediate purpose. However, other teams last for years and are pennant winners every season. The most successful often become Old Boy (and, increasingly, Old Girl) networks. Such networks are good if you are on the team, and of course, bad if you are not. Teams tend to limit, or at least control, competition *among* the members while directing competitive energies toward solving problems. You can improve your prospects for survival by being on a winning team.

SECTION 17: PERSEVERANCE

Perseverance is one of the most powerful combat skills. It is critical to overcoming obstacles—especially if the obstacle is too big or too hard for easy solution. Keep working away at something that does not immediately yield to your initial assault. Use "salami tactics." If the whole thing is too big to handle all at once, then slice off one bite at a time. When you finish that small, manageable piece, take another slice. Break huge tasks into small chunks.

If a frontal attack is out of the question, try turning the flanks. Maneuver around the obstacle to one flank or the rear. Attack from a new and unexpected direction. Consider, for example, that if you march forward to the front of the enemy's line, you face forty or fifty rifles. But if you attack the enemy's flank, you face only one.

The point is that on the battlefield you must keep trying, and trying, and trying. The ancient Chinese observed that, "Water is the softest of all things. Yet, with time and perseverance, it can wear away even the hardest of stone."

SECTION 18: SACRIFICE

Sacrifices will be necessary. Normally in life we have to give up something to get something. What do you want? And what are you willing to give up to get it? Every organization expects aspiring employees to "pay their dues." That means taking an assignment in Newark or Bujumbura in order to be competitive for the job in San Francisco or Paris. Or working nights, or weekends. Or separations from the family.

So pay your dues. But make sure you get a receipt: Make sure that your sacrifice or achievement serves the organization's highest goals and is duly noted. Your "receipt" could take several forms. It might be special mention in your annual appraisal, a certificate of achievement, a Letter of Commendation, an award, or other recognition all noted in your official file and on your résumé. Most valuable of all is acknowledgment by senior management, whether formal or informal, of your special achievement. This will also help build what is called your "corridor file" which is your *informal* personnel record—your professional reputation. We will discuss "corridor files" near the close of this section.

SECTION 19: BATTLE FATIGUE

The workplace, as numerous books and articles attest, is fraught with tension, stress, worry, fear, and confusion. After all, it's a battlefield. Expect, therefore, to suffer battle fatigue. Battle fatigue, unfortunately, is a natural consequence of the workplace, and is all too common. It can make you tired, drained, and stressed out. You may become overly irritable and jumpy, and may find your thinking impaired. Worst of all, your self-confidence may be eroded. If you don't believe in yourself, who else will? Sadly, as these mental and physical conditions mount, your ability to perform decreases rapidly. Then battle fatigue becomes even worse.

The key is to rebuild your confidence in yourself. Do the obvious. Rest. But don't just rest. *Think* about the experiences that brought on your battle fatigue. Analyze what went right—and why—and what went wrong—and why. Can you identify specific conditions that contributed to your battle fatigue? Can you change or overcome these conditions? Reflect on what you might do differently to delay the onset of battle fatigue in the future. Then, work yourself back into the line by focusing on a mastered skill. Keep busy at things you do well and enjoy doing. Success, however small, is good therapy. Dealing with battle fatigue is a key survival skill.

SECTION 20: TIME

Managing time effectively is another vital combat skill. Wise use of time is the ability to do the right things first.

You should be more judicious about spending your time than your money. Shakespeare's *Richard II* ruefully remarked, "I wasted time, and now doth time waste me." Waste your time and you waste your life.

Time is the most valuable of all resources. It is a non-renewable resource. It is beyond price. As the Chinese sages observed, "An inch of time is an inch of gold, but an inch of gold cannot buy one inch of time." Wise use of time is essential if you are to be well-positioned to seize opportunities.

In 1781, George Washington seized one such opportunity which proved decisive. Washington learned in August that a powerful French fleet intended to sail to Chesapeake Bay to confront Lord Cornwallis and the British Army. Washington immediately realized that victory was possible if he could move rapidly overland from New York with the combined French and American armies. Washington knew that if he moved too slowly, Cornwallis might receive reinforcements or manage to escape. Washington spared no effort to reach the lower Chesapeake while the French fleet was still in place, and Cornwallis was vulnerable. By September, Washington's land forces were in position, and

CONDITIONS OF THE BATTLEFIELD

Cornwallis found himself trapped between French naval guns and French and American siege artillery. Of critical significance was the fact that the British supreme commander in New York—who could have saved Cornwallis—dithered and delayed until 17 October. On that day, Cornwallis raised the white flag, and two days later surrendered at Yorktown—the act that ended the American Revolution and assured American independence.

Napoleon Bonaparte, possibly the greatest captain of modern times, also recognized the value of time to operations. Napoleon once told an aide, "You may ask me for anything you like, except time." The truth of Napoleon's own maxim is shown in the hour of his great defeat. In the battles preceding Waterloo, with Wellington and Blucher weak and separated, Napoleon procrastinated, thereby enabling Wellington to build up his forces and Blucher to recover from a tactical defeat. At Waterloo itself, Napoleon failed to commit the Imperial Guard at the moment it was needed. Thus, Napoleon's Prussian and British enemies succeeded in combining their forces, the battle was lost, and Napoleon's empire passed into history. It is clear that wise use of time can mean the difference between victory and defeat.

The beginning is the most important part of the work.

Plato
The Republic

The next thing most like living one's life over again seems to be a recollection of that life, and to make that recollection as durable as possible by putting it down in writing.

Benjamin Franklin

FOUR

THE PAST IS PROLOGUE

SECTION 21: THE RECORD

The legacy of performance, whether good or bad, is a track record—a kind of history. Whether we speak of the racehorses at Pimlico, the New York Yankees, or the Fortune 500, all have their track records. Those records are a rich mix of gains and losses, ups and downs, victories and defeats. While many Americans might agree with Henry Ford that "history is bunk," they nevertheless seem fascinated by track records and statistics. Fact is, the written record is how most people decide which racehorse to bet on, which stock to buy, and which person to hire or promote.

Since you will be compared with your peers—just like a racehorse at Pimlico—you need to build the best record of which you are capable. Build a solid professional history based on superior performance at each job you hold. Although consistent excellent performance is not by itself the guarantor of success, documented achievement is essential to your advancement and professional growth.

SECTION 22: DEFINE REQUIREMENTS

Careful documentation of performance is vital, but there is a hidden first step. That step is to have management define, in black and white, exactly what it expects of you on the job. Some organizations are very good about this. You will receive a Letter of Instruction (LOI), Terms of Reference (TOR), Advanced Work Plan (AWP), or similar document laying out what you are to do in varying amounts of detail.

Some organizations, however, are not so good at this. It is your responsibility to know what you're expected to do. So if you receive no written guidance, draft your own LOI and have your boss approve it.

Never agree to an LOI that directs you to do things you cannot do. If you lack the competencies, the resources, or the authority to do something, don't agree to be held responsible for doing it. Be sure you know the deadlines—and whether you can meet them. Remember, it is this document that will define the criteria by which you are evaluated. It's a binding agreement. Therefore, take care that your LOI is something you can live with.

Your LOI should change over time. Indeed, you should ensure that the LOI is expanded as you take on new responsibilities. If you are assigned new work, or duties requiring more effort or skill at a higher level, make sure your LOI is amended to reflect these changes. If you are doing more, you should be given due credit for doing more.

SECTION 23: OFFICIAL AND "CORRIDOR FILES"

Your personal track record at work consists of two parts: your "official file" and your "corridor file." You will carry both throughout your working life. Both are important.

Your official file is, of course, the documentary record of your performance. In theory, it consists of performance evaluations for each and every job you have held in a particular organization. Usually, such evaluations are written by your supervisor every year, or every time your duties change substantially. After you've been with an organization some time, your official file will become fairly thick.

Be sure you personally review your official file regularly. It should contain everything you want it to contain: performance evaluations, commendations, copies of diplomas and certificates, records of training, and a continually updated biographic profile. You are your own best career management officer; it is *your* responsibility to ensure that your history is complete and accurate. Never depend on a personnel officer to do this for you.

There is also your "corridor file," and it may differ from the paper file—substantially, in fact. Loosely defined, your "corridor file" is how you are perceived by others in the organization. It is your professional reputation. Your "corridor file" may or may not outweigh your official file, but it *will* contribute to personnel decisions affecting you, such as consideration for promotion, reassignment, or specialized training.

In some ways a positive "corridor file" is more important than your paper file. If you have a reputation for hard work, split rail honesty, intelligence, and a cheerful disposition, you will be amazed how many doors will open to you. The paper file will merely confirm what others already know: you are someone they want on their team.

By the same token, there are folks around who concentrate exclusively on burnishing their paper credentials while conducting themselves in a highly negative manner toward their fellow beings. Rest assured that sooner or later their actions will come back to haunt them. After a while, the people around these paper creatures will come to know their tactics fairly well, and neither the bosses nor the rank-and-file will be deceived for long. Beware if you follow this course of action—having a stellar paper file, but a deservedly bad reputation. A rotten fish will smell no matter how beautifully it is wrapped.

SECTION 24: HELP THE BOSS HELP YOU

A final thought is to help your boss help you. Well before the boss's evaluation of your performance is due, prepare a summary of your achievements for the boss. Don't be shy. If you did something really well, mention that fact. It is especially wise to link your achievements with the organization's central goals: higher profits, better services, new products, and so forth. How did your work contribute to the attainment of these goals? Don't exaggerate your contribution, but at the same time, don't underestimate yourself and your work. If credit should be shared, say so. It shows that you are honest and appreciate the importance of the team. Your boss will likely appreciate your thoughtful labor-saving summary. And your final evaluation, not surprisingly, will strongly resemble your input. You're on your way.

KEY POINTS OF PART 1: PERFORMANCE

- As a professional, you are captain of your own career.
- Most career successes are built on solid records of performance—the consistent delivery of desired results.
- Results are achieved through determined, stubborn effort.
- Performance is vital, but not sufficient by itself.
- Perseverance is essential to overcoming obstacles.
- Like it or not, you are a competitor. Your work will be constantly evaluated and compared with others.
- Inventory your talents and abilities.
- Talent only has value when transformed into achievement. Show what you can do.
- Make wise use of your time—do the right things first.
- You are your own best personnel officer.

PART TWO: RELATIONSHIPS

Serious occupation is labor that has reference to some want.

Hegel

Circumstances rule men; men do not rule circumstances.

Herodotus

FIVE

THE HUMAN CONDITION

SECTION 25: THE ORGANIZATIONAL PERSONA

"What a piece of work is Man," wrote Shakespeare. What a piece of work, indeed. By turns, we humans are clear-thinking and pig-headed, nobly generous and narrowly selfish, intensely loyal, incredibly capricious. It wouldn't be so bad if we could cleanly separate the Black Hats from the White Hats. Alas, with the exception of Mother Teresa, we all wear hats of gray. As the popular cartoon character, Pogo, once said, "We've met the enemy, and they is us!"

Poets and philosophers have debated the human condition for centuries. And will for centuries more. What concerns us here is the human condition *on the workplace battlefield*.

Perhaps the place to start is with that human creation most reflective of human nature: the organization. Organizations are, like their creators, clear-thinking and pig-headed, generous and selfish, and almost everything else we humans are. Why should this be so? Because organizations are inhabited by humans. Humans establish them, humans own them, humans direct them, humans work for them. Organizations take on the characteristics of humans.

Consider the church choir, the Communist Party, the Continental Can Company, or the CIA. Each organization reflects the wishes, hopes, fears, needs, interests and goals of its members—and especially of its leaders. Nearly every organization goes to great lengths to portray itself as caring and concerned—even altruistic—toward its members and those it serves. One sees in the corporate propaganda phrases such as "employee-centered," "empowered employees," and "managing with a difference." These slogans are intended to give the impression of a nurturing organization. But unless a bonafide saint heads your organization, you would be well advised to view these pronouncements with skepticism. Never trust an organization to do anything more—or less—than serve its own interests.

Ultimately, each organization develops a distinctive "persona." Indeed, chameleon-like, managers and employees over time take on the color of their organization. There is a subtle process of Organizational Darwinism at work, a process of "natural selection" which causes some to stay, some to go, some to move up rapidly, and others to stagnate.

Do you find the organizational "persona" congenial to your own? Or not? This is a very important question. Like the survival of other species, your survival depends on your ability to adapt to the local habitat. If you can't adapt to the local habitat, it is better to look elsewhere for greener pastures.

SECTION 26: KNOW THE UNWRITTEN RULES

Many organizations have a code of unwritten rules. Be sure you know and observe them. Violation of taboos of certain tribes in New Guinea or the upper Amazon might cost you your head. The same may be true if you flout the taboos of your organization in New York, Chicago, or Washington. For instance, some insist that men wear white shirts with red ties, others that employees speak and act deferentially to managers and schmooze on Friday afternoons with the bosses. Still other organizations desire that you contribute to, or support, pet projects sponsored or endorsed by the organization. None of this will be written, of course. Thus, you need to be something of an anthropologist to gain insight into your organization's culture and its shibboleths. All have their distinctive culture and customs.

SECTION 27: WHO WANTS WHAT

Now let's examine the landscape of the organization itself, for the organization is *on* the workplace battlefield, and at the same time, it *is* the battlefield.

The key to understanding an organization is to understand who its various inhabitants are, and what they want. It is the people and their wants which form the basis for relationships. Remember never to confuse an organization with the individual human beings who inhabit it. It is not the organization *per se*, but *people in the organization* who hire, promote, train, transfer, and fire. And they do so for a variety of motives including interests, expectations, jealousies, fears, personal agendas—and a host of other reasons.

However "noble" Man might be, he is nonetheless motivated by wants. Many are zealous for their own advancement, fame, or fortune while secretly (or not so secretly) jealous and resentful of others' successes. Many crave public recognition. Indeed, Napoleon marveled at how men would willingly die for a small piece of ribbon called the Legion d'Honneur. "Management"—however that may be defined—has devised all manner of motivational schemes to capitalize on human wants. Positive motivational schemes range from knighthoods to free refills at the local pizza parlor. Negative motivators include such things as a fine on overdue books—or the threat of a firing squad, as the case may be.

Perhaps, then, in its most elemental form, the human condition in the workplace is the interplay of needs and motivation.

In the workplace, you will hear of "the carrot and the stick." Management freely uses both to obtain results from its staff. Common rewards include certificates, cash bonuses, decorations, and promotions. Obviously, sticks include reprimands, docking of pay, and reductions in grade. The point is that it is not the actual fact of reward or punishment, *but the expectation thereof* that motivates. If a person expects that by taking some action he or she will be rewarded, it is likely that action will occur. By the same token, expectation of punishment for failure to perform in an acceptable manner can motivate certain individuals.

Organizations usually employ a mix of carrots and sticks. Some organizations tend to use negative motivation more heavily than positive motivation, while others prefer positive incentives. Just be sure you know what the ground rules are before you play.

Possibly the two most powerful words in the English language are "I want," for from these words come great inventions, incredible achievements, enormous sacrifices, heinous crimes, and daily activities.

What is it that a person wants? Discover this, and you are in position to motivate.

Remember, too, that *everyone* has wants, not just you and me here in the trenches. The corporate president must show the Board "results" if he hopes to hold his chair. The sales manager needs to show an upward curve if she hopes to win promotion to the Chicago office. The general must win the war if he wants to be Chief of Staff.

Find out what the various people in your organization want. Are you in a position to help others achieve their goals? If so, you have just acquired a measure of power, and you'll find the human condition at your command.

Consider the following situation. The Board of Directors wants to see great sales figures. That is the reason the corporate president (who reports to the Board) focuses heavily on sales. You, as regional sales representative, have increased the company's sales and revenue. You have given the president what she needs and wants (namely, the ability to show the Board healthy sales figures). You and the president are by no means equal in rank or power, but you have just attained a measure of power over her. The president knows that she cannot afford to lose you—at least not now. Thus, you will find the president remarkably receptive to your suggestions and requests because they are directly relevant to the goals *she* needs to achieve.

Mere unassisted merit advances slowly, if—what is not very common—it advances at all.

Samuel Johnson
1709–1784

If a man does not make new acquaintances as he advances through life, he will soon find himself left alone. A man, sir, should keep his friendships in a constant repair.

Samuel Johnson

SIX

WHO YOU KNOW

SECTION 28: NETWORKING AND MOBILITY

How often we've heard, "It's not what you know, but who." What a cliche. Alas, the cliche is true. Actually, it's both *what* you know *and who* that count. But if there is a well-connected moron competing against an unknown genius, guess who'll get the promotion? The relationships you develop in the workplace augment your demonstrated competence by giving you *mobility*. With enough vines, even the inarticulate Tarzan could move quickly through the thickest jungle.

Networking is vital to career advancement. Used offensively, a network helps you capture opportunities which might otherwise be beyond your grasp. Defensively, your contacts provide a safety net in times of adversity or outright career disaster. At all times, your network of relationships gives you the indispensable battlefield resources of intelligence and communications. Intelligence is vital to understanding what is going on, and communications is essential to reaching key individuals and groups in your organization and elsewhere.

Most often, we hear of networking as a relationship between peers—and perhaps only between peers of the same gender. Let's expand our thinking. We know that organizations consist of a wide variety of people. If there are cooks, account executives, file clerks, executive assistants, and graphic designers in an organization, there should be cooks as well as account executives—and all the rest—in your network of relationships. If there are gray-haired old Baby-Boomer geezers of 50 and GenX employees of 20 in an organization (and all manner in between), you should develop contacts with these people as well. Put simply, you need to reach as far into the organization as you can manage. And into other organizations—even competing ones.

Admittedly, some relationships will prove more valuable than others. Some individuals can give you valuable insights into the politics and daily operations of the organization. Some can give you timely warning of threats or opportunities. Some can broker introductions to key individuals. And some can promote you and give you the job in Paris. But great or small, all relationships are important. Indeed, it is the network itself which has supreme value to you, not any one member of it.

SECTION 29: OF MENTORS

Much has been made of "The Mentor." This Gray Eminence is supposed to take you by the hand, lead you safely past all the terrors of the workplace, and set you at last upon the Corporate Throne.

Actually, it's not that simple. True, some few lucky individuals have had their careers made by a single guiding hand. But not many. More often, people move through their careers with the help of many hands—and not all of them hands of great power. Of course, if a Gray Eminence stops by your desk this afternoon to take your career firmly in hand, by all means, rise and follow!

More realistically, what you need is a wide range of relationships with those who know you, know what you have done, and know what you can do. The fact is that in the course of your career, key individuals in a position to help you often retire, die, or get transferred to Cleveland. This is bad news, indeed, if you have placed all your career eggs in just one Mentor basket.

SECTION 30: BUILDING YOUR PORTFOLIO OF RELATIONSHIPS

So how does one develop a wide range of relationships? First, remember that some relationships are tactical. That is, they are highly focused on a single objective and of short duration. Then there are strategic relationships. These are long-term, based on shared interests and the attainment of broad, fundamental goals.

Why should two individuals form a relationship? Simply put, because it is in their mutual interest to do so. Each member gains something from the relationship—that is, the relationship fills recognized needs. By the same token, should either member believe that the relationship no longer fills needs, the relationship will dissolve.

Obviously, "intangibles" such as shared religious or political beliefs, abstract values, outside interests such as hobbies or sports, or a shared experience, all serve to pull people together. Personal friendship and genuine admiration may precede or follow a professional relationship. Often, professional and personal aspects of a relationship blend to such an extent that they are hard to distinguish from one another. In most cases, this is not a bad thing. Friendship is usually coupled with respect, and the two conditions make harmonious and productive teamwork possible.

But also bear in mind that there can be dangers as well. In some cases, too close a personal relationship can lead to highly unprofessional conduct. Caution, good judgment, and ethics must be your guides.

Remember that professional relationships have professional reasons. Both parties need something the other can supply. Your demonstrated ability to perform is a powerful motivation to others. The greater the boss's need, the stronger the relationship will be. The same is true of peers, subordinates, and others in—or out—of the organization. Remember that other people are most easily recruited into your network of relationships if they believe you could be useful *to their own* ends.

SECTION 31: KEEP FRIENDSHIPS IN REPAIR

Sadly, wallflowers are seldom winners. You must go out and develop your own relationships in the business world, academe, government service, politics—everywhere. The point is that relationships won't develop on their own. You must invest the time and effort to meet people, and work hard at developing solid relationships with a wide variety of people.

Young people often misunderstand the purpose of clubs, social organizations, fraternities, athletic associations, and the like. While tennis or chess may be the ostensible reason for the club to exist, a club's main purpose is to bring people together. Many successful people make excellent use of memberships to establish and maintain valuable professional relationships.

The club or association, however, is merely the backdrop. What is important is the activity on stage. And that is the formation of friendly relationships which may last a lifetime. Each relationship is formed individually. Although they may take months to develop, relationships can be destroyed in minutes. They require constant thought and care to maintain. Tact and empathy are the hallmarks of healthy interpersonal relationships. You must understand each friend's likes and dislikes, personality type and values, special interests and concerns, talents, and background. And, above all, you must understand your friend's needs.

It also doesn't hurt to gain insight into your friend's links upward and outward. While your friend may share many acquaintances and contacts with you, he or she almost certainly will know people you do not.

Now let's apply a little math to this concept. Let's suppose you can count in your circle of acquaintances just one hundred people who know you fairly well. (Most people know far more than one hundred people.) Let's suppose that each of these good people also have their own circles of one hundred friends—people whom you do not know. Potentially, you can be in touch with up to 10,000 people. How? These friends of friends serve as referrals. But only if you work at maintaining your own network of friendships.

It is up to you to maintain your portfolio of relationships. Keep them in good repair. Visit or look in on people. Call or write to them. Expand your network of relationships at every opportunity. Always remember that a healthy relationship is a two-way street. Be sure you deliver what is expected of you. But also make sure that a relationship is serving your best interests, and taking you in the direction you want to go.

A final thought concerns ethics in relationships. While relationships should serve your best interests, you must bear in mind that you do not have the right to advance your personal interests at someone else's expense—any more than they have the right to advance their own interests at your expense. Avoid exploitative relationships; strive for partnerships.

All the world's a stage,
And all the men and women merely players.
They have their exits and their entrances;
And one man in his time plays many parts.

Shakespeare
As You Like It

... If all men count with you,
but none too much ...

Kipling
If

SEVEN

KNOW THE PLAYERS

SECTION 32: ALL GOD'S GRUNTS

As you maneuver forward in the workplace battlefield, you will meet a wide variety of other grunts out there—a bewildering variety. Some dogfaces will be just like you—wearing the same uniform, in fact. Other grunts struggling along will be very different. They look different. They talk differently. They wear different uniforms. They sometimes eat funny food. Study each grunt carefully.

Whatever their individual differences—tall, short, old, young, fat, skinny—they all have important battlefield roles. Basically, we will see bosses, peers, retirees, secretaries, admin types, and others in and around the trenches.

SECTION 33: BOSSES

In the workplace, the single most important relationship you must manage is that with your immediate supervisor—The Boss. Bosses come in all shapes and sizes, and with an infinite variety of personalities and temperaments. Bosses have different interests and agendas. But they all have specific needs. As we've discussed, it is vital for you to determine what these are.

There is no argument that the ideal boss is congenial and intelligent, a good listener, and takes an interest in you. Some are like this, but sadly, too few. Treasure them.

The majority of bosses are very ordinary human beings. They have their share of foibles and shortcomings. They are decent enough folks, but often are wrapped up in their own concerns. You will work for many such people.

Unfortunately, there are also some truly "bad apples" out there. These bosses are arrogant, abusive, foul-mouthed, sneering, scheming, and duplicitous—and these may be their good points. Despite thousands of company dollars squandered on "management training," and hours spent giving them lectures on "building employee relations" and "effective communications," these guys are—and will forever remain—west ends of eastbound horses. Avoid them.

The great majority of bosses are not visionaries, nor even strategic thinkers. Most are driven by mundane tactical, day-to-day concerns—namely, their in-boxes and e-mail. Many are harried by *their* bosses. Many have short memories—which is another good reason you should document your performance well. While some bosses are as sharp as razor wire, others are as dumb as fence posts. And perhaps as productive.

Get to know the strengths and weaknesses of both the exceptional and the merely ordinary bosses. Even the very best have weak areas. Learn what the boss must do to satisfy his/her boss. *How can you help your boss be more effective?* If possible, make yourself indispensable. If you can help your boss look good, *you* look good.

Remember that bosses are people, too. They have many of the same problems you have: leaking pipes, flat tires, overdue bills, bratty kids, and unfulfilled ambitions. As Irish folk wisdom has it: "We all have our troubles." You have yours, they have theirs. Be observant and try to understand the reasons why your bosses act as they do.

Tact and diplomacy are essential ingredients of success in managing your relationship with the boss. Even if the boss is as dumb as a rock, you cannot act like a mining engineer ready to blast. Manage differences of opinion carefully and diplomatically.

Now, if you get stuck with Captain Ahab, it doesn't take much to see you have a crisis on your hands—a crisis that could very well lead to a career disaster. So, if you can't live on board the Pequod with the boss, lose no time in gathering wood for your raft. Escape from his/her ship at your earliest opportunity. If you have applied some of the lessons of this book, you will already have a network of relationships to help you make your escape.

The point is, choose your bosses carefully. You have to live with them.

SECTION 34: PEERS

Now look around you in the workplace and you will see a lot of other people just like you. They may be the same age. They may be the same pay grade. They may even do similar work. These are your peers.

Your peers constitute a natural group in which you will want to build relationships. And, it is relatively easy to do so.

There is probably no relationship quite so strong as that which spans many years. Childhood friends. College roommates. Army buddies. "I knew him (her) back when ...." You come to know a lot about a person over twenty or thirty years of association. You may develop unquestioned trust. You certainly know what you can expect.

From the opportunity standpoint it could be a very long time before anyone in your peer group reaches a key position, if ever. Even so, peers are enormously helpful in obtaining valuable information, and in providing connectivity with other groups and organizations. Your peers may know where the jobs are, or where opportunities may be opening up. They also are a source of support in bad times, and companionship in the good times.

SECTION 35: SECRETARIES AND ADMINISTRATIVE ASSISTANTS

Never, ever, *ever* discount the influence of a secretary. A good secretary or administrative assistant will *always* know what is going on. Indeed, a secretary may very well know better than the boss! The secretary serves as gatekeeper for the boss—and can get you in or keep you out with equal facility. Remember that secretaries or admin assistants keep the calendar and schedule appointments. They are well-positioned to put in a good word for you, and they know where the opportunities—as well as the minefields—are located.

Moreover, a secretary serves as a surrogate communicator and is, in fact, trained to transmit full and complete messages to and from the boss. "Keepers of the secrets," secretaries are a vital part of your network. Administrative assistants often support entire offices, not just the bosses. They handle functions that make life easier for you and for many.

Don't take either for granted. Show appreciation and respect for their skills and contributions.

SECTION 36: RETIREES

Retirees form a specialized group associated with an organization. These are good people to know for the history and lore of an organization. They can explain why Bottomly hates Bigelow. They often can provide shrewd advice: "Stay out of the Bigelow-Bottomly battle." They are sources of training and expertise. Get that expertise if you can. Remember that retirees have a lifetime of experience and skills, and many are quite willing to pass their knowledge along, if asked.

However, one must also remember that retirees have limited—and declining—reach into the organization. Most gave up power when they gave up their responsibilities. Though some retirees may retain residual influence due to personal prestige, or through their remaining network of relationships in the organization, they represent the past, not the future.

SECTION 37: AND OTHER RANKS

Other players—admin people, trainers, account execs, cooks and bottle washers—see parts of the world you may not see. Treat everyone with respect. Whatever their work or rank or interests, all are human beings. They also have important work.

We tend to ignore and often fail to appreciate people who are different from us. But, so what if they wear a different uniform than we do? They are worth knowing—and befriending. You never know when one of these people might be vital to accomplishing a task. Then the truth of the ancient axiom once more will be proved: "Better to have and not need, than to need and not have."

During World War II, the "Mighty Eighth" Air Force in Europe was justly proud of its top pilots. But without the unsung mechanics and ground crews, the planes would never have left the ground. Imagine the situation if there were only pilots and no mechanics.

By befriending many peers, bosses, retirees, secretaries, and other ranks, you accomplish two important goals. First, you widen your network of contacts while increasing your effectiveness at getting things done. At the same time, you are boosting morale in your organization by showing respect for others. Thus, by building solid working relationships, you advance your own agenda while leaving your organization a better place than you found it.

SECTION 38: SAME FACES, DIFFERENT PLACES

Bear in mind that during a career you will see many of the same faces again and again. You can never predict who you know today that you will run into at some future bend in the road. Since people move at different speeds in their career paths, you may well end up working for some of these people.

We win our friends not by asking favors, but by doing them.

Thucydides

A friend in need is a friend indeed.

Benjamin Franklin

EIGHT

ASSESSING THE COSTS AND BENEFITS

SECTION 39: PAY FOR WHAT YOU GET

Except for sunshine and fresh air, everything has a cost. Relationships certainly have a cost. The coin in which this cost is paid may vary: effort, expertise at a critical moment, information, influence, a key favor–you name it. However, not surprisingly, the benefits you hope to derive from your relationship are similar to what you paid—namely, expertise at a critical moment, information, influence, or a key favor.

Remember that the core of a relationship is mutual interest. Unless the relationship has other underpinnings—such as shared beliefs, family, or friendship—it will end as soon as it brings no further benefit to one or both parties.

Professional relationships are continually subject to cost-benefit analysis, even if subconsciously. If a relationship is vital to your interests, it is likely that you will return phone calls promptly, get together for lunch often, pay attention always, and deliver what is expected consistently. If that tie should weaken, you may still be on good terms, but somewhat less prompt in answering your phone calls and going to lunch. And, if a relationship proves to be a valueless time-burner, you likely will stop returning calls entirely.

SECTION 40: PATRONAGE

At the top of the relationship list is patronage. This is usually a relationship between a superior and subordinate. Patrons are distinguished from well-wishers (which they may also be) because patrons have clout—and they are willing to use it on your behalf. Patronage in a bureaucracy can resemble a European feudal system. You are assured of protection and preferential treatment. But in a time of invasion or crisis, you will be called upon to fight on behalf of your patron. And if your patron goes down, you may well go, too.

A patron is someone in your direct chain of command who has come to depend upon you and who, in turn, has tangible rewards and benefits to give. Patronage used to be more prevalent in the workplace than it now is. But despite its gradual erosion by so-called "transparent" systems of reward, patronage still exists and makes its influence felt in assignments and promotions. Watch which officers follow their patrons from post to post.

A mentoring relationship is more profound than is a patronage relationship. More than simple dispensation of rewards and perquisites to faithful followers for loyal service, a mentoring relationship is based upon conscious teaching and counseling over a protracted period—perhaps the best part of a career. Unlike a patron, a mentor systematically grooms and prepares a novice to assume high position and responsibility.

Many organizations talk a good game about mentoring their employees. Be advised that few organizations walk the talk. You are more likely to encounter patrons than mentors.

SECTION 41: INTELLIGENCE

Next in value is intelligence. Never fail to tap into the flow of information regarding people and organizations. You don't do this by reading the Company Bugle. Although faintly useful, the organization's news rag is as bland and carefully edited as Beijing's *People's Daily*. Rather, you obtain information from those who are on the scene, and indeed, from those who will make the decisions. This requires solid relationships with both peers and superiors. But good intelligence is well worth obtaining. Without it, you are limited to a worm's eye view of people and events.

The best intelligence is not that which recounts what happened. It is, rather, the accurate reporting of *what will happen and why*. It is "actionable intelligence"—that is, intelligence which can be put to immediate, or near-term use. Actionable intelligence in the workplace battlefield, therefore, is not mere office gossip. It is information that allows you to make decisions and take actions that determine outcomes favorable to you. Thus, true intelligence is distinguished from gossip because it enables the possessor to anticipate threats or opportunities.

There are two kinds of actionable intelligence—battlefield and strategic. Battlefield intelligence enables you to capitalize on tactical opportunities; strategic intelligence gives you the power to capture opportunities brought about by long-range trends. Strategic intelligence helps you anticipate the major directions in which your organization is headed. Many organizations claim to reinvent themselves every four or five years. Phrases such as "re-engineering" do not apply to the production line but to the corporate culture across the board. The accelerated pace of change which has hit the American workplace has brought with it a great deal of career development pain. If you can read the tea leaves of major change in your organization—and reinvent yourself to keep pace—you will be well positioned to seize opportunities which many others cannot even envision.

Remember that the highest quality intelligence is of little value unless you use it wisely.

SECTION 42: FAVORS

A favor at a critical moment may be vital to your success. In traditional China, a "face" relationship was based upon the iron-clad obligation to reciprocate for favors received. Not being able to reciprocate—that is, not to return a favor—was said to "lose face." You must pay your debts if you hope to retain your credit rating. Only the very naive would expect that they owe nothing for a favor asked and received.

Examples of favors might include the following: access to a key individual, a recommendation or endorsement, help with a project, coordination of a document or presentation, "greasing the skids" for a major activity. As wise old Ben Franklin observed, "A friend in need is a friend indeed."

The system keeps count. "I owe you one." "You owe me one." These are debts to be paid, not empty greetings. When another player taps you to "call in some chits," be prepared to deliver. After all, a ways down the road, *you* may need to do the same. You'd better be credit-worthy.

SECTION 43: DAMAGE CONTROL

Damage control is another important benefit that flows from maintaining healthy relationships. In a thirty-year career, you can take it to the bank that at some point you will experience rough sailing.

Damage comes in many forms. It could be a project with which you were closely associated—gone sour. It could be a sudden move to cut the workforce—starting with you. It could be the vengeance of an old enemy who has emerged from his sewer to blacken your name. It could be plain old bad luck—you were at the wrong place at the wrong time.

To weather the storm you need to call upon elements of your network. Do you need to escape from Ahab's ship before it goes down with all hands? Have you dug yourself into a pit over an ill-advised project? Are you in a tailspin due to downsizing, with you being the one sizing down? Alert your network at once. A good "corridor file" will aid your cause immeasurably as it opens doors. Move your official file or résumé adroitly through those open doors. Use your network to set up the interviews you need. And afterwards, remember to say "thank you" to each and every one who helped you in your time of need.

SECTION 44: PROTECTION FROM ENEMIES

Finally, protection from enemies is a real benefit. As the saying has it, "Friends may come and go, but enemies accumulate." You *will* accumulate enemies. Just try to accumulate them as slowly as possible. And for heaven's sake, don't go looking for enemies! The Crusades went out with the thirteenth century. But when enemies emerge—whether spurred by envy or fear, or a clash of personalities or interests—arrange defensive measures through your network. Better to have your enemies battle uphill against well-prepared positions than to have them catch you unprepared and defenseless in the open.

Defensive alliances are key to your survival, for an enemy who fights alone or outnumbered risks defeat. Most enemies are sensible enough not to risk conflict when defeat appears likely. Even so, you would be wise to avoid giving ammunition to your enemies. Don't say things that can be used against you. Don't do things that you may later regret. Be cautious, maneuver carefully, keep your defensive alliances strong.

The eminent nineteenth-century statesman, Lord Palmerston, handled Britain's foreign interests in Europe, Asia, and America, with the skill of a chess master. The consummate pragmatist, Palmerston stated that "Britain has neither permanent allies, nor permanent enemies—only permanent interests."

Lord Palmerston's dictum about "no permanent enemies" is not quite true in the workplace. There are indeed permanent enemies (just as there are transient interests). But, as the teams shift and new alliances form, stay on good diplomatic terms with as many as possible. Remember that, in most cases, relations are not personal, only professional.

And sometimes, with patience and hard work and luck, you may achieve a truly great victory by turning an enemy into a friend. Always assess your enemies with just as much care as you assess your friends. Enemies have wants, too. Perhaps, without compromising your own interests, you can bring about a diplomatic coup by winning over an opponent.

KEY POINTS OF PART 2: RELATIONSHIPS

- Organizations reflect the characteristics of their human inhabitants. Find an organization in which you can survive and grow.
- Know the organization's unwritten rules, and follow them.
- Discover what someone wants—particularly your boss—and you are in position to motivate. Successfully address these needs—be of value to your boss—and you become indispensable.
- Remember that bosses are people, too. Deal with them diplomatically.
- Relationships give you mobility, intelligence, and communications channels in the workplace. Build relationships and alliances and maintain them for both proactive and reactive purposes.
- Mutual interest is at the core of a relationship. Know what you need, and what you can give in return. Make sure you return favors and say thank you.
- The single most important relationship you must manage well is that with your immediate supervisor.
- Obtain actionable intelligence to help you anticipate threats and opportunities, and to stay ahead of the currents of change in an organization.
- Don't put all your career eggs in one mentor basket.
- Never discount the importance of showing respect for everyone in your organization. Over a career, you will see many of the same faces again and again.

PART THREE: OPPORTUNITIES

In the fields of observation, chance favors only the mind that is prepared.

Louis Pasteur

Consider the little mouse, how sagacious an animal it is which never entrusts its life to one hole only.

Titus Maccius Plautus

NINE

RECOGNIZING OPPORTUNITY

SECTION 45: WHAT IS AN OPPORTUNITY?

His wife and children had died. His opera had failed. Sick at heart, convinced that he was a failure, he was on the point of giving up composition altogether. However, recognizing the man's talent, the canny director of Milan's La Scala Opera House asked him a favor. Would he give his opinion about a libretto? He did, and stayed on to write the music that became the powerful opera, *Nabucco*. The man was Verdi.

How narrow a turning point was that favor. Had Verdi given up music, his name would be obscure at best, and perhaps unknown. More significantly, we might never have had the chance to hear and enjoy *Rigoletto*, *Il Trovatore*, *La Traviata*, or *Aida*. And Italians would not have had Verdi's lyrical—and stirringly patriotic—music to spur them on as they struggled to free their country from foreign oppression.

Recognition of opportunity is vital because opportunities come in a bewildering variety of shapes and sizes. Some may not even seem to be opportunities. What is an opportunity? How would you know an opportunity if one appeared? Is it agreeing to look over a libretto? Receiving a baseball bat at a Catholic boys' school? Being flatly told "it can't be done" and then sailing into the unknown?

As with Verdi, some opportunities arise from a desire to conquer adversity. As with Babe Ruth, some opportunities arise from a determination to win the respect of others. And, in Columbus's case, opportunity arose from an intense belief in himself—that he *could* discover Cathay by a new route.

Clearly, opportunities come in many forms. Some opportunities are obvious. Others, less so. Still others are lucky breaks—pure happenstance. But opportunity is not totally a creature of chance. Even the lucky break would not be so lucky if the individual were incapable of making the best of the break. "Chance favors the prepared mind," as Louis Pasteur noted.

And this brings us to the central point. Opportunities are not so much fate, chance, or luck as they are a convergence of external circumstances and internal drive and determination.

The dictionary defines opportunity as the "right moment to take action toward a definite goal." But this definition makes too much of timing. What is the "right" time? Tomorrow? Next month? Five years from now? Rather, what is more important is *recognition of the circumstances* in which your unique knowledge, skills, or talents can be put to use toward a definite goal. And even more importantly, it means *preparing yourself today* for that favorable combination of circumstances.

SECTION 46: ALTERNATIVES AND OPTIONS

Up to this point, we have looked at opportunity as a one-dimensional concept. Let's make it multi-dimensional. Plautus observed that it is a wise mouse that has more than one mouse hole. Options and alternatives may be considered opportunities in many dimensions. The lesson, therefore, is to always generate alternatives. When one option fails, there are others.

A set of alternatives or options, like a choice of mouse holes, enables you to move in any of several directions if and when the need arises. In a very real sense, you are preparing your own opportunities.

How does this apply on the workplace battlefield? To generate alternatives—a range of options—you need to be alert and make good use of your network of relationships. As mentioned, these are people who know what you can do. Even if you are happily and steadily employed, you would be a wise mouse to develop a multiplicity of possible holes. Remember that the workplace is by nature chaotic and its future highly uncertain. What seems firm and sure today may be gone tomorrow. Don't wait for downsizing or reorganization to start thinking about alternatives. By then, it's too late.

As you have learned, your network is in a position to spot opportunities for you—and sometimes even *create* them for you. Consider for a moment that the director of La Scala could easily have let Verdi return to his native village unhindered. Instead, he gave Verdi a libretto which (he correctly suspected) Verdi would turn into a masterpiece.

Maybe it's not 100 percent true that we make our own luck. But it *is* true that we and our friends—those who believe in us—generate most of our own opportunities.

While we stop to think, we often miss our opportunity.

Publilius Syrus

Art is long,
life short;
judgment difficult,
opportunity transient.

Goethe

TEN

PREPARING FOR BATTLE

SECTION 47: BATTLE PLANS

Only a fool would go into battle without a plan. Since you are too smart to make this elementary mistake, we will now turn our attention to planning.

All plans are developed with reference to a clearly identified objective. Capturing Hill 629 or the district sales manager's job in Greater Houston are both examples of clear objectives. We must presume that either goal is realistic and attainable given the particular resources you bring to the battlefield. In the case of Hill 629, you will need artillery and infantry. In the case of the sales manager's job, you will need a sterling performance record—and a first rate network of relationships.

Having selected the objective—whether it is tactical and immediate, or strategic and long-term—begin to plan for its attainment. The planning process, curiously, is "backwards." Start with the objective. What conditions must exist in order to assure capture of the objective? Then ask, what must be done to create those conditions?

The next step is to consider possible strategies for creating the conditions required. This would include examining various plausible routes to the objective, and likely obstacles and enemy reactions you will encounter. Careful thought is given to each of these considerations.

Last, after appraising the advantages and resources at hand, soberly appraise your gaps. Can you obtain the needed additional resources? If not, can you somehow use other advantages or resources to compensate for those you lack? Remember: base your plans on sober appraisal—not wishful thinking.

And critical to your plan of battle, how can you play to your strengths while hitting your opponents where they are weakest?

Count Helmuth von Moltke, the brilliant strategist and soldier-scholar who headed the Prussian general staff for thirty years, was correct when he said that all battle plans change with the first shot. But, if you are as smart as Plautus's mouse, you will have devised a pocketful of alternative plans that can be activated if needed. Never go with a single, rigid plan. Be flexible. Develop fallback plans. Visualize—and game out—alternative scenarios.

With battle plans in hand, you now are lying in wait for opportunities. *Better, you are developing your own opportunities that lead on to your objective.*

When conditions are ripe—exploit them rapidly. Make a rapid calculation of risk. Be decisive. Hit hard and continue to move on—don't stop. This is the critical moment of victory or defeat.

SECTION 48: TACTICS AND WEAPONS

Now, to the tactics of the workplace battlefield. We've discussed the employment of networks and the use of official and "corridor" files. Three other weapons at your disposal are the résumé or curriculum vitae (CV), the interview, and the testimonial. All can be employed skillfully as part of your overall scheme of maneuver.

SECTION 49: RÉSUMÉS

You will receive tons of advice on the "proper preparation" of a résumé. Seek details elsewhere. Merely bear in mind that Gypsy Rose Lee's advice regarding the proper length of skirts applies to résumés. Both should be "long enough to cover the essentials, short enough to be interesting." Don't oversell yourself. Don't stretch the truth. Be brief. Use the résumé as you would battlefield leaflets—to get out a succinct, truthful message about your professional competencies, work experience, education, and objective.

A résumé and a curriculum vitae have the same basic purpose: each exists to sum up your career to the present. Put another way, both documents showcase your career achievements and professional skills. Résumés often present a chronological account of professional achievements, education, and brief personal information. Although a CV presents much of the same information as a résumé, it is more tightly written, contains less detail, and focuses more heavily on professional skills. Use a CV with those who know you (they need a brief aide memoire, not a history.) A résumé probably is in order if you are trying to reach organizations and individuals who do not know you.

Whatever your profession, you must maintain a high ethical standard. Be truthful, even if the temptation is great to be dishonest in order to win a tactical point. Your long term loss is your reputation. For sooner or later, people will come to know that you were dishonest. Once lost, your credibility as a reliable and trustworthy person cannot be regained.

SECTION 50: INTERVIEWS

The interview, be assured, is *your* weapon if you choose to use it. It is your opportunity to convey your message directly to the interviewing panel. Since the interview is a golden opportunity to amplify on the CV, the file, and whatever else the interviewers already know about you, don't be ambiguous. Don't stammer and beat about the bush. Don't rehash stuff they already know. Say exactly what you want to say. Remember, it's *your* show. Yes, they will have questions. So? If you *really do have* the experience and track record you claim on paper, the interview will be a piece of cake. A walkover, in fact.

Some people are naturals at interviews. They look sharp, they present themselves well, they have the Gift of Gab. These fortunate few can interview successfully for almost any position.

Most of us need a little preparation. Choose your ground carefully, focusing on areas where you are familiar with both the substance and the players. Think through possible questions and responses. Most importantly, jot down a few "talking points" to use during the interview. These talking points will enable you to move the discussion in directions more or less of your choosing. Unless you have the Gift of Gab, it is never a good idea to wing it when an opportunity is at

stake. Know what message you wish to leave with the interviewers—and make sure you leave it.
- Anticipate questions
- Be prepared
- Convey self-confidence
- Dress appropriately

SECTION 51: TESTIMONIALS

If additional firepower is needed to carry the day, have it available. You can call in some favors and draw on relationships for timely testimonials in the right quarters.

There is absolutely nothing wrong with gentle self-advertisement. Naturally, you are your own best advocate. Make personal contact whenever possible. But it is perfectly acceptable to bring in third parties to testify to your excellent qualities. Here, your network of relationships can prove exceptionally helpful.

They serve as references. References, in effect, authenticate that you *really are* what you claim to be on paper. "Well, my buddy, Jack, whom I've known since we were crickets in a cornfield, says you're OK." It's kind of like word of mouth advertising with you as the product.

Consider using testimonials from among selected members of your network of relationships *before* key interviews. If you are "well and favorably known" to the Vice President for Research and Development, it cannot hurt you to have VP/R&D mention you favorably to the VP for Sales who is seeking candidates for the sales rep position in San Francisco. Even if you don't get the job at this time, your name will be remembered and the endorsement will weigh in your favor. There will always be other times, other opportunities.

SECTION 52: KNOW YOUR TARGET

You should ideally get to know each interviewer personally, if you are unacquainted. This gives you some direct insight into their personalities and interests, and also showcases you. You become something more than just another name on a piece of paper.

However, you should also develop intelligence on each interviewer through trusted sources who can give you additional information on that person's background, special interests, expertise, and likes and dislikes. Secondary sources often serve as a "sanity check" on your own impressions. Moreover, they may be able to give you information about the interviewer's personality, and details about his or her history and background beyond those which you obtained yourself.

In addition to collecting information via your network of relationships, go to the library. Look at trade journals or professional listings. Nearly all interviewers would be impressed to know that you took such an interest. A little research can also make you better informed than the rest of the pack.

SECTION 53: OPENING THE CAMPAIGN

Remember to have a "loose-tight" plan of action built around attainable objectives. Interviews, résumés or CVs, and testimonials should be carefully integrated into your overall battle plans. They are not used piecemeal or in isolation. You should know your objective and line of march before you open the campaign, and prepare your tactics to support the operation. But once you decide on battle, don't flinch.

And one thing more. Your mental attitude is critical to the outcome. Every combat commander knows that the will to win is vital if his soldiers are to prevail in battle. The same applies to you. Put on the armor of courage and optimism. Do not doubt for a moment your capabilities. Resolve to win.

Fortune favors the brave.

Virgil
Aeneid

There is a tide in the affairs of men
Which taken at the flood, leads on to fortune.
Omitted, all the voyage of their life
Is bound in shallows and in miseries.

Shakespeare
Julius Caesar

ELEVEN

NOTHING VENTURED, NOTHING GAINED

SECTION 54: TAKING RISKS

If opportunity's brain is generating options, surely its heart is taking risks. Risk is an essential part of advancement. Indeed, it is an element of nearly all significant decisions you will make in life.

Risk is the inescapable element of making decisions in uncertain situations. Willingness to take risks is surely one of the toughest combat skills to learn. When the situation is perfectly clear, all factors understood, and all outcomes known, decision is easy. Indeed, it's a no-brainer because it is risk-free.

But in most high-stakes situations, not all the facts may be known, much less understood. The outcome is far from clear—indeed, it may be obscured by the smoke of battle and filled with hidden perils. Things could go wrong. Time is short. Available information is contradictory. Yet a decision must be made.

The problem affecting risk is obvious. We always want to win, but what if we *lose*? Taking risks brings out uncomfortable gnawing feelings. We tend to dither, to procrastinate, to put off decision—indefinitely, if we can. Let's face facts: most of us prefer to avoid risks entirely.

Yet the cost of avoiding risk is assuring failure.

Consider Babe Ruth. Few ball players struck out as often as he did—more than 1,300 times, in fact. But when his bat connected with the ball, the ball likely went out of the park. Every time the Babe swung his bat, he was taking a risk. Three strikes and he went back to the dugout.

But the key was that Babe Ruth was not afraid to try—*and indeed to fail*. For in his magnificent willingness to risk the hoots and jeers attending a strikeout, he also experienced the exhilaration of hitting home runs.

It's important to understand *and accept* that where risk is concerned, setbacks *will* occur. You *will* strike out now and then—maybe often.

SECTION 55: REDUCING UNCERTAINTY

Now, it's important to understand that Babe Ruth didn't swing at every pitch thrown, only the ones he judged to be "good." And "good" he measured by his eye and hand and batting experience. The Babe took *calculated* risks. And so should you.

There is a canyon of difference between wild gambles and calculated risks. The difference between a gamble and a calculated risk is the degree of uncertainty. A gamble rests on pure chance, whereas a calculated risk can be given a weighted probability (i.e., 50-50, 60-40, 80-20, etc.) based on available information.

In all uncertain situations, it behooves you to reduce risk by reducing the degree of uncertainty. You wouldn't buy 100 shares of Ajax Widget without gathering some information about widgets in general and Ajax in particular. By the same token, use your network of relationships to collect information on job offers, business offers, prospective bosses—in fact, anything on the battlefield. Don't expect to remove all the fog and smoke. Uncertainty will remain.

But by reducing uncertainty, you can bring the law of probability into play in your calculation of risk. Karl von Clausewitz would be proud of you. Clausewitz wrote that "A great part of the information obtained in war is contradictory, a still greater part false, and by far the greatest part somewhat doubtful. What is required of an officer in this case is a certain power of discrimination, which only knowledge of men and things and good judgment can give. The law of probability must be his guide."

SECTION 56: DECISION

With risk assessment accomplished, you must move to decision. Lose no time. Be decisive. Grit your teeth—and jump. A workable decision that is timely—even if it has flaws—is preferable to a polished, flawless decision that is too late.

Remember that decisions—whether good or bad—are positive. Good decisions lead to fame, fortune, victory and glory. Bad decisions, at least, lead to good experience. The aftermath of a bad decision is not a time for discouragement, but for reflection. Discouragement leads nowhere. Reflection leads to wisdom. And ultimately to better decisions.

Remember, too, that even failure can be positive. Disappointment, frustration, and anger often result from setbacks. You can allow these reactions to harden into sterile bitterness. However, channeled positively, disappointment and frustration can ignite powerful, creative efforts that propel you in radical new directions in your life and work. Never fear failure. It may be the essential ingredient of your eventual success.

Consider the fate of Handel's oratorio *Messiah*. Far from being an instant success, *Messiah* was poorly received in London in 1742. Despite this initial failure, Handel did not for a moment doubt *Messiah's* worth, and he lived to see his faith in the work justified. Between 1750 and his death in 1759, Handel performed *Messiah* as a fund-raiser for charity. In the words of one historian, *Messiah* "fed the hungry, clothed the naked, (and) fostered the orphan." Today few who hear the soaring majesty of the "Hallelujah" Chorus would doubt that *Messiah* is one of the finest musical creations ever written. It is worth noting that *Messiah* was not published until well after Handel's death. But imagine our loss if Handel, in disgust, had torn up his manuscript immediately following the disappointing London performance.

There is greatness in failure and disappointment when there is the commitment to persevere, to struggle on despite the odds.

It is a rough road that leads to the heights of greatness.

Seneca

Those who know how to win are more numerous than those who know how to make use of their victories.

Polybius

TWELVE

YOUR MOVE

SECTION 57: CONSOLIDATE

Congratulations! You got the position. But success imposes new responsibilities. Before you hold your victory party and break out the bubbly—consolidate your position, scan the field anew, and start thinking about possible future moves.

Immediately set about building an enviable record of performance in your new job—acquiring new professional skills and experience. Immediately start building an addition to your network of relationships. And, begin preparing the ground for spotting and capturing opportunities as they arise.

Master the new job as quickly as possible. If you don't know something, sit down with someone who does. Don't try to bluff your way through. Learn, practice, and master. Remember that there is no substitute for solid performance in each job you hold.

Take time for others. First, get to know your subordinates (if any). Second, get to know your boss well. Third, get to know your peers and others. Healthy relationships are essential to your performance and for reasons of mobility, intelligence, and communications.

Learn as much as possible about your new organization. Study its divisions and subunits, its field operations and headquarters, its prospects and problems.

Learn about other organizations which interact with yours. These may be friends or foes, suppliers or customers, allies or competitors.

Keep your eyes open. Keep your bags packed. You never know when you'll run across the opportunity of a lifetime, or need to escape from a sinking Titanic before the waves close over you. If you're prepared, you can move out on a dime.

SECTION 58: LEADERSHIP AND RESPONSIBILITY

Leadership and responsibility go hand in hand. Probably no ability is more praised—or as rare—as leadership. Probably no other commodity commands as high a price in the job market as responsibility. This is because responsibility is the highest form of risk. It is the willingness to make decisions of great consequence in the face of great uncertainty. When senior CEO's are wrong, corporations fall and employees lose their jobs. When commanders fail, armies are destroyed and soldiers lose their lives. As you progress through your career, you should seek positions of leadership carrying increased responsibility as you feel yourself able to bear its weight.

Awesome as responsibility may be, it is the wellspring of great undertakings. It is the very essence of leadership, which inspires others with a grand idea or vision and carries that vision through to conclusion despite a sea of troubles.

Responsibility and visibility often go hand in hand. Visibility is essential to the expansion of relationships. Responsibility is vital to professional growth. Thus, you should seek a job which is "too big" for you—and highly visible. This is not to say that you should strive for jobs for which you have few qualifications and little aptitude. It is to say that you should push the limits of the expertise and skills you do have. Indeed, the new position should force you to grow professionally—and you must have the willingness and ability to learn new skills and acquire additional valuable experience. This clearly is taking a calculated risk. If you succeed in your venture, you will grow into the job, and the visibility you enjoy may even make you famous. And if you fail, at least people will respect you for daring greatly.

SECTION 59: THE ME-WE TRANSFORMATION

There is one final consideration before we close. That is the transformation from "me" to "we" as one advances through a career. One of the biggest hurdles for young people is understanding that above the entry level it is essential to work through others. Indeed, the "me-we" transformation is for many the major dividing line in one's career.

At the "me" level, one's own work is key. This is how you establish your record of performance. But at the "we" level—the various levels of management—you achieve your work through the efforts of others. You will be judged on the results achieved by your unit.

The transformation from technical specialist to management generalist is not easy. Some specialists cannot delegate tasks. Others prove unwilling or unable to trust subordinates with real responsibility. And a few others, sadly, become intoxicated with their newfound authority and status. The trappings of power become all-important for these people, and they thirst for more power in order to gain even more lavish perks. Worse, their behavior may deteriorate to the point where these scoundrels become the next generation of the eastbound horses we so despise.

Hopefully, you will not follow the example of these workplace wienies. Your agenda is broader than stepping on others or reveling in the trappings of power. But if not, at least you will serve a positive end as another bad example.

Beware of the trappings of power. If you are at least a little bit embarrassed by the private office, plaque on the door, and reserved parking space, your instincts are in the right place. Now, there is nothing inherently "wrong" with any of this as long as you are willing to accept the cost: long hours (often an average of three hours per day more than the rank-and-file), decisions you may come to regret, frustrations about projects and programs gone awry, tedious and seemingly endless meetings, and other cares and worries too numerous to mention.

All this goes with the territory. No one said that the yoke of leadership was easy, or the burden of responsibility was light. Just remember to earn your perks every day.

The best move you can make if you become a supervisor is to treasure your people. This is not only good and worthy in itself. It is eminently practical. It doesn't take a management guru like Peter Drucker to tell you that a subordinate who is treated well is also likely to be productive and motivated. Shower credit, praise, and rewards on your bunch—and they will react like thoroughbreds at Pimlico. Invest in your people—give them training, new areas of responsibility, broader experience. Seek their ideas. Be honest with them. Believe in your employees and they will reward your faith in them.

Remember that you are planting trees for the future. Help your people reach for opportunities. After all, they are trying to grow professionally—just as you did.

SECTION 60: FOLLOW ME

When it comes time to move on, do so gracefully and without rancor. You have prepared the way for others to follow. Those who follow will remember your example, your helping hand, and your friendly word, and will multiply your good influences in their lives, in their organizations, and in American society. Leaving the world a little bit better than you found it is the mark of the true professional.

KEY POINTS OF PART 3: OPPORTUNITIES

- Opportunities come in many forms. The trick is to recognize the circumstances in which your knowledge, skills, or talents can be put to use.
- Always generate options and alternatives.
- The cost of avoiding risk is ensuring failure.
- Remember that even bad decisions can lead to good experience.
- Never fear failure: it may be the essential ingredient of your eventual success.
- Leadership is the ability to inspire others with a grand idea or vision, and carry that vision through to completion despite a sea of troubles.
- Responsibility is the willingness to make decisions of great consequence in the face of great uncertainty.
- Getting the new job or promotion isn't the end, but a new beginning. Continue to grow, develop, and treat others with respect.
- Your most important duty is to leave the world a little bit better than you found it.

CLOSING THOUGHTS

SQUARE ONE

We have been together now through sixty sections of *Career Combat*. You are now ready for battle in the American workplace. At this point, you must carry on the campaign by yourself. "Fortune favors the brave," as the Roman poet Virgil reminds us. Still, the examples and maxims in this manual can be of daily use. Don't allow this FM to gather dust on your shelf. It was designed for hard use in the field. The greatest compliment you can pay to the book is to use it.

In closing, I want you to understand clearly that my own path was hardly smooth. It has had many blind alleys, wrong turns, unpleasant bumps, and disappointments. What is important is that you should not have to repeat my errors in order to learn how to build a successful career. "Wise men learn from others' mistakes," according to the Chinese sages. After all, I wrote *Career Combat* expressly to help you avoid the painful "trial and error" method of building a career that I went through.

But alas, mistakes are often an important part of the learning process. It is recorded that a young man once asked an old man the secret of his success. The old man rubbed his chin, thought, and then replied sagely: "Good decisions." Impressed by this, the young man asked the old man how he made good decisions.

Again the old man thought deeply and said: "Experience." Now thoroughly impressed, the young man pressed on eagerly and inquired how the old man came by his experience. Again, after some thought, the old man replied solemnly: "Bad Decisions." It is important that you don't give up after making a few mistakes, though. It is also said that "nothing in the world can take the place of persistence. Talent will not; nothing is more common than unsuccessful men with talent. Genius will not; unrewarded genius is almost a proverb. Education alone will not; the world is full of educated derelicts. Persistence and determination alone are omnipotent."

My message in *Career Combat* is for newly-graduated high school and college students, servicemen and women separating from active service seeking opportunities, middle-aged employees who find themselves stagnated in their careers, workers who gave the best years of their lives only to be shown the door following downsizing or corporate mergers, and for women and minorities entering or re-entering the American workforce. The six-figure execs can take care of themselves. They frankly don't need this manual because they have already mastered the art of building their careers. But for the rest of you, my great hope is that you have found in *Career Combat* a map and a new battle plan that will help you solve the day-to-day challenge of staying alive on the workplace battlefield. And more importantly, I hope you have found the courage to do so.

With every good wish for your success,

Alex

NOTES